KNIT ONE, HAIKU TOO

Maria Fire

Adams Media
Avon, Massachusetts

Published by Adams Media, an F+W Publications Company
57 Littlefield Street
Avon, MA 02322
www.adamsmedia.com

ISBN 10: 1-59337-571-9
ISBN 13: 978-1-59337-571-3

Printed in Canada.

J I H G F E D C B A

Library of Congress Cataloging-in-Publication Data
Fire, Maria.
Knit one, haiku too / by Maria Fire.
p. cm.
ISBN 1-59337-571-9
1. Knitting. 2. Haiku. 3. Fire, Maria. I. Title.

TT820.F52 2006
746.43'2--dc22

2006014707

This publication is designed to provide accurate and authoritative information with regard to the
subject matter covered. It is sold with the understanding that the publisher is not engaged in ren-
dering legal, accounting, or other professional advice. If legal advice or other expert assistance
is required, the services of a competent professional person should be sought.
—From a *Declaration of Principles* jointly adopted by a Committee of the
American Bar Association and a Committee of Publishers and Associations

Many of the designations used by manufacturers and sellers to distinguish their product are
claimed as trademarks. Where those designations appear in this book and Adams Media was
aware of a trademark claim, the designations have been printed with initial capital letters.

This book is available at quantity discounts for bulk purchases.
For information, please call 1-800-872-5627.

"The Way It Is" Copyright ©1998 by the Estate of William Stafford. Reprinted from *The Way It Is:
New & Selected Poems* with the permission of Graywolf Press, Saint Paul, Minnesota.

KNIT ONE, HAIKU TOO

Of Suffering and Delight

I discovered the broad magic of knitting when I was eight years old. The year I turned fifty, I was still knitting. That was the year my mother died and I learned to write haiku. I found the way of knitting and the way of haiku have much in common. Both teach focus, patience, and presence in a baffling world of suffering and delight. Both revel in the beauty of the "turn"—whether it's at the end of a row of knitting or at the end of a line of haiku. Both practices help me loop my life together.

The glide of my hands
In my knitting I am free
It is my ocean

A Yarn

"Yarn" can mean a strand of twisted threads used for knitting. It can also mean a long and entertaining narrative filled with adventures and lore. I hoped to write this book as a poetic and philosophical journey through my knitting life. Once I spun my yarn, I discovered I had knit myself into yet another shape. Whether you are a shape-shifting knitter or not, may the words I have poured through my heart and hands bring you pleasure. May they incline your own heart toward tenderness for yourself and the challenging life you face. I believe in the work we each do, that it serves those who came before, those who are with us now, and those who will come after.

With the words and yarn
How will I dance the right step?
Mystery leads me

All We See

As a child I read that Helen Keller knit.
I put on a blindfold and felt my way through my
house. For Helen, was all color black? Did the
tap of her knitting needles pulse like a butterfly
wing close at hand? Perhaps she felt the tex-
ture of yarn and smelled its odor more acutely
than a sighted person. Today I cast my eyes
down to look at my own knitting. What grace to
see, in whatever way, creation's beauty.

Ineffable force
My unique experience:
Together we knit

She Bet Right

In 1960, the summer after second grade, Mrs. Warwick moved in next door. We lived in a small town in the heart of North Carolina. When Mother lay down in the afternoon to nap, I slipped out to visit. Mrs. Warwick and I sat in the heat and humidity on her porch swing. My legs dangled from the wooden seat. Hers anchored us and kept us rocking with an even back-and-forth rhythm. Mrs. Warwick fed me lemonade and oatmeal cookies. She taught me to play canasta with the cards lying in our laps. One day, she laid her cards down. "I bet you would like to knit," she said. She bet right. Mrs. Warwick knit year round. Even in the summer heat. Otherwise, she said, she would get too grumpy and do harm. She gave me needles, undyed cotton yarn, and taught me the knit stitch. She did my casting on. Then I knit a lumpy square she described as a dishcloth, with the perfect knobby texture for scrubbing counters and plates. That summer, the making of dishcloths consumed me. I gave one to every adult I knew.

Yarn looping in yarn
Tactile and magical, like
Two sticks make a fire

Tough Grits

Mrs. Warwick's husband often complained about minor things. When he did, she muttered under her breath, "Tough grits!" Grits are corn that has been soaked in lye to become hominy, dried, and then ground. It boils up to a consistency like cream of wheat. As a child my dad ate "South Carolina Ice Cream," a treat made with white corn grits, milk, and sugar. I preferred yellow grits, salted and buttered— polenta by another name. Those grits were crayon yellow, the color of sunshine, the color I would have preferred knitting my washcloths in. Instead, Mrs. Warwick, quite generously, gave me tough cotton yarn, dull beige, like dirty dishwater. "Tough grits!"

Lacking the color
Find poetry in stitches
Making-do is joy

Along Came a Spider

Spiders, our original knitters, appeared on Earth 310 million years ago. Some spider silks are five times stronger than steel. Sometimes my yarns fray or split apart in my fingers. Yet, when I knit them, a certain shape holds and flexes without tearing. I never understand this miracle of tensile strength.

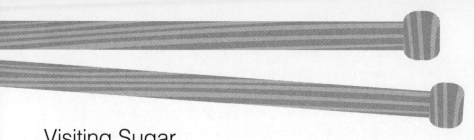

Visiting Sugar

The week before I started fourth grade I visited my grandfather Sugar, Sug for short. When I handed him two of my knitted dishcloths, he held them up and beamed. Then he hung them by his sink. He said he would use one for dishes, the other to wipe down the table and countertop. Sug said knitting was an excellent skill and a "soothing habit," or so he'd been told. His mama had knit clothes for him when he was a little boy, and I could learn to do the same. In his widowed retirement my grandfather had moved to live by a muddy lake in the red clay pinelands of North Carolina. Sug didn't talk a lot, but what he said counted. And he listened to me. He baked pound cakes without recipes and let me drink hot tea with milk served in my grandmother's china cups. When we caught catfish from the lake, he made stew.

Afternoons we spent hiking through the woods around Sug's house. I took short, quick steps to keep up with his long strides. In the evenings we sat on the porch and watched the sun set. At dark I switched on a lamp so I could knit, and I asked my grandfather to recite poetry. He knew long passages of classical poems by heart. Much I didn't understand, but his sonorous voice wrapped the night around us—and my busy fingers danced to the music of his words.

Warm words in night air
  Pine smell and needles clacking
Oh, sweet obsessions!

Wool Gathering

Poet C. D. Wright calls the unknown place that exists before creation "the area of darkest color." Magic always begins with a something that is nothing. One night I dream I am in an open field of grazing sheep. The sky is a blue that pierces the eye. Suddenly, puffs of wool are floating down around me. I hold my hands out to catch them and rub snatches of wool between my fingers. I say, "The possibilities are endless!"

The Kindness of Her Hands

Growing up I didn't see much knitting going on. Besides Mrs. Warwick, the only other knitter I knew was Zilphia, who attended my parents' Presbyterian church. She walked to services from her house two blocks away, her white hair always clamped in circles with bobby pins. The visible outlines of her scalp formed a pink mosaic. I could study it during sermons. Mostly, however, I watched her knit.

I'm not sure anyone spoke to her directly about it, but I heard my father and other elders say it was irreverent to knit in church. When I peeked during our minister's boring, endless prayers, Mrs. Zilphia was knitting. She carried her work in a green brocade bag that had two large and circular wooden handles.

Following church every Sunday, Mrs. Zilphia turned from the pew in front of me and took my hand in hers. She held it cradled between the palms of her hands. I hated when she let go. I always asked her to show me what she was knitting. Her children, grandchildren, and great grandchildren kept her busy making complicated projects. "She can knit anything," I thought.

On a Sunday shortly after I turned nine years old, and shortly before she died, I blurted out, "I want to knit like you."

Mrs. Zilphia took each of my hands separately in hers, turned them, and examined them closely. She looked me in the eye and said, "These are the hands of a strong knitter."

Yielding her secrets
Wise woman casts a future
Quivers on my skin

Knitting for the Brain

Our hands are made to be sensitive givers and receivers.
The density of nerve endings in our fingertips is manifold
compared to the rest of the body. Neurophysiologists say
that using our hands stimulates cellular development in the
brain. This further justifies hours of knitting. While I luxuriate
in this pleasurable touching, I am performing gymnastics that
strengthen my brain!

Where Babies Come From

When I attended Girl Scout camp at age ten, we slept eight to a cabin in four bunk beds. The summer nights were warm and humid, and we used flashlights to visit the outhouses, or latrines as they were more delicately called. We ate meals cafeteria-style, and when finished, we cleaned up after ourselves. We swam in a muddy pond, played horseshoes, shot archery, and wove lariats (not as good as knitting, but a decent substitute). I was gloriously happy until the night my cabin-mate Prudence and I argued about where babies come from.

Earlier in the year, my mother had been pregnant with my youngest sister. Because I relentlessly pestered my mother about *how* she became pregnant, she gave me a blue book called *All About Being Born*. She told me to read it, that it would answer all my questions. Included were elaborate sketches of female and male "reproductive organs." When I finished the book, I knew not to ask questions, but whenever girlfriends whispered about baby-making, I proudly shared what I knew. One of the nights at camp in that tenth summer, an opportunity presented itself. The air was thick and hot. I was glad to be on a top bunk, level with the screens and the slight puffs of air filtering through them. Six of the girls were clueless about the birds and bees. That left it completely up to Pruddy and me. I held forth in the dark. I used all my new words like "vagina" and "insemination" and was rewarded with the sound of indrawn breaths. "Absolutely wrong!" Pruddy announced. "All babies come out of a woman's right thigh. Up on the inside."

"No, they don't," I said.

"Yes, they do!"

Pruddy played her ace. She announced that her father was an obstetrician. More indrawn breaths. Without my blue book on hand, I lost the battle. That night, the vote was seven to one in favor of the high-thigh delivery theory.

How much it mattered
Threading love through this new seed—
Little dance inside

Scout's Honor

I never "flew up" to become a Girl Scout. I did spend two years as a Brownie. I didn't care much for the light cocoa-colored uniform and beanie, but I loved time spent with art projects. In the fall of my second year, our leader, Mrs. Kirkland, decided we would learn to knit. I was honored to be the assistant teacher. Mrs. Kirkland brought in wool to make nose warmers for Christmas presents. First, we knit triangles. Then we folded them in half and seamed smaller triangles into pointed cones that would stretch over noses. We cut short lengths of yarn that we knotted into tassels for the tips. For each nose warmer, we braided two strips long enough to tie in a bow at the back of the head. In the spirit of the season, Mrs. Kirkland gave us red, white, and green yarns. I knit more nose warmers than any other troop member. Mixing three colors into tassel, tie, and cone combinations, I developed five different versions, one for each family member, except my youngest sister, who was still a baby. On Christmas Day, my brother put his nose warmer on his head, tied it under his chin like a birthday hat, and jumped up and down on the sofa. My one-year younger sister said hers made her look like Rudolf—the reindeer. My parents said, "Thank you," but didn't put theirs on. The rush of creation was now distant memory. I suddenly realized I didn't like my own warmer—the itchy feel on my nose, the way the ties slid down my head, or that close, damp breath from sucking air through the wool.

When I described nose warmers to my husband Calvin, he thought I had dreamed them up. On the Internet I found postings that touted the pleasures of knitting and wearing nose warmers. I did enjoy my experience of knitting them. However, a few days after that Christmas, I threw my presents away. No one ever mentioned the missing nose warmers.

Step in a puddle
Jubilee of small mistakes
Wandering with yarn

Two Mismatched Mittens

My decade-younger friend Kay, who lives in northern Minnesota, grew up on a farm, the third girl before at last a boy child was born. "They tried to teach me to knit at home, but I couldn't learn." I'm jealous that she was formally taught to knit in a seventh grade home economics class. Her first project was a pair of mittens. She was so proud when she finished. There was only one problem. One mitten fit her brother. The other fit her dad.

Mixed-up Muse

The head Greek god Zeus birthed Athena, goddess of the practical arts, not from his thigh, but from his head. What interests me more are the nine female muses he sired with Mnemosyne. Muses exist for the sole purpose of helping humans excel in the arts and sciences. The irony is, muses intercede to give artists the wrong ideas. Turns out, it takes wrong ideas to generate the right ones. This comforts me. The abandoned babies, all those projects I toss or hide in my closet, are essential to the full process of creating my vibrant masterpieces.

Grace of our failures
Life consolable again
The hands still dreaming

"The folklore among knitters is that everything handmade should have at least one mistake so an evil spirit will not become trapped in the maze of perfect stitches. A missed increase or decrease, a crooked seam, a place where the tension is uneven—the mistake is a crack left open to let in the light."

—from the essay "Yarn" by Kyoko Mori

To Every Season

As a lifetime knitter, I have started many projects I never finished.
And whether in a funk or frenzy, I confess that I periodically shamed
myself and labeled my knitting a "waste of time." I gave away stashes
of yarn and my collection of needles, only to decide I must knit again.
Repeating seasons have finally fostered a trust in the fallow spaces
of my not-knitting. Like the mother bird who builds a new nest each
spring, when my time is right, I pick my needles up again. But if by
chance I should forget, three friends have promised to shout, "Stop!"
if they see me leaving home with plastic bags of sundry yarn in hand.

Dumpster Diving

Since his mid-teens, my young friend Tucker has been a connoisseur of Dumpster diving. He showed me a wonderful library book on the topic and directed me to some Web sites. I'm enthusiastic about his idealistic salvaging, which lessens waste of undamaged goods otherwise headed to the landfill.

My mother was a Dumpster diver before I ever heard the term. She was inventive in many ways. On good days, she provided us with joyful entertainment. In our spare kitchen with no counter space, she once knocked a hole in the wall, put a picture frame around it, and nested our toaster there. She won a washing machine through a magazine contest and then fashioned wire coat hangers around the agitator to transform it into a dishwasher. She used it that way only once. The spin cycle proved problematic.

My father was trying to build a business from scratch, and we had no cash flow in our household. At some point, however, Dad managed to get a loan for a station wagon, perfect for Dumpster diving. I was the painfully aware age of twelve. My two younger sisters and one brother seemed oblivious to any impropriety on our parts. Yet when we drove around behind the stores downtown, I was the one Mom hoisted up to peek inside the large brown Dumpsters. Somehow I was certain we were breaking the law and would be caught doing it.

I became a convert to Dumpster diving the day Mom stopped behind McClellan's, a local family-owned department store. At the top of the Dumpster I saw multiple hanks of yarn in iridescent colors. I scrambled inside the Dumpster and tossed them out to Mom. I heard her laughing as she gathered them into our station wagon. "Maria, these are all for you!" she said. No one else in my family knit.

Wildish colored yarn
As showy as a peacock
Shimmy, shimmy, pop!

The Friend on a Hanger

My Minnesotan friend Kay says in seventh-grade home economics class she chose a miniskirt pattern for her second knitting project. "It had a zipper and everything." Not only that, she knit it in a Fair Isle pattern using "truly fluorescent colors." Over thirty years later, the skirt is still in her closet. Who could throw away something like that? I would use it like a magic wand and pull it out to spark up my life when youthful exuberance ran low.

Time Will Pass

In the ninth grade, Mr. Grimes taught me math, some sort of algebra. He didn't really teach math, however. He lectured about life, and most specifically about World War II. Mr. Grimes never said he was a veteran, but he often repeated the story of "a man he once knew" who was captured and held in a German prisoners-of-war camp, locked in a dark cell and never allowed outside to exercise. There was only a cot to sleep on, and no books or companions. Mr. Grimes said the thing that saved that man's sanity was the complex mathematical equations he imagined and worked out in his head.

The large round clock on the wall above the blackboard was taped over with a piece of construction paper. On it, Mr. Grimes had written in large block letters, "Time will pass, will you?" Mr. Grimes was dark and thin with a perpetually pinched face. He paced the room as he lectured. He didn't drone. His voice crescendoed and fell with an agitation that made me anxious.

In the gray of that winter I started my first cardigan with a green yarn my grandmother picked "to match" my green eyes. All of it would be knit in simple stockinette stitch, but there would be buttonholes for fancy brass buttons. As an antidote to his edgy monologues, I began to sneak my knitting into Mr. Grimes's class and worked with it under my desk. To appear attentive, I looked up now and then. As my sweater grew, I grew less cautious. The fateful day came when Mr. Grimes stopped his pacing right beside my desk. "Class?" Mr. Grimes announced. "Miss Fire seems to have found the way to save her sanity." I looked up with dread. Mr. Grimes was grinning.

Gleeful knitting hands
Stitch, an endless beginning
Blow away the dust

Leaving Home

It was 1968. I wanted to escape my family, my town, and my country. I wanted a new world. I was a junior in high school about to turn seventeen. The American Field Service (AFS) exchange student application asked for countries I preferred. I wrote, "I will go anywhere." Perhaps I was sent to Denmark because the previous summer I had studied two semesters of German at a local college, and Danish, like English, is a Germanic language. The first month in my new country, I crammed to learn Danish with nineteen other young Americans. We boarded in a small village on the island of Fyn, birthplace of Hans Christian Andersen. I was living a fairy tale! Bente, our DSL (Danish as a second language) teacher was short and wiry. Her salt and pepper hair was mown down to the scalp. I had never seen such a thing, and I loved it. During breaks from classroom study, I sauntered over to the post office or bakery. The baker always broke into a broad grin when I tried my Danish. "May I ask for—?" I said, and then pointed to a pastry in the glass display case. Through four weeks, Mr. Hansen patiently taught me to pronounce the name of all his goodies. "A thousand thanks, and goodbye," I mispronounced each time I left. A little bell tinkled on the door as it closed behind me. Except when she stood to write or draw something on the chalkboard, Bente sat in her chair and knitted during our language lessons. She was working on a complex sweater using at least four different colored yarns that she moved in and out, at anytime, on any row. Even more puzzling, instead of throwing the yarn over the needle from the right, she was mysteriously pulling it from the left. I didn't understand why or how. Later, in my new home, my Danish sister Lone would teach me this "continental" style of knitting. Lone told me I knit in the British style, really much slower "and so inefficient."

Knitting from the left
And that throwing from the right,
Both pull to center

Different Strokes

For years, I passed on my Danish sister's advice that the best way to knit was the continental method. Teaching English style was easier, but I warned each novice knitter they were learning a slower method. Two women in my Naughty Knitter's group disagreed. Elizabeth, who grew up in Alabama, held her left needle pointing straight out, knob at her waist. Yarn flew from the right and stitches whipped into shape like a machine was producing them. Margaret, who learned to knit in England as a five-year-old during World War II, always buys extra long metal needles. She tucks the left one under her arm and proceeds. I sat beside her so we could knit in tandem. It seemed she did knit faster. I mentioned "combined knitting," where some people knit continental method and then purl back using British style. The group groaned. Okay, we agreed, each knitter must perfect a unique practice. Like painters, we develop original strokes—up, down, and wherever around.

"Curve: the loveliest distance
between two points."

—Mae West

Turn on Point

Going to live in Denmark at seventeen was not just a curve for me, but an abrupt turn. I shot down a chute and popped out two years later with life expanded beyond my wildest dreams. I grew fluent in another language, found a new loving family, and felt the connectedness of humankind, despite differing worldviews. As if that wasn't enough, I had been planted in knitter's heaven. I lived in the beautiful port town of Kalundborg, in the crotch of a fjord located on the opposite side of the island from Copenhagen. Around town I saw all ages knitting, and I spent whole school days doing the same. I attended a "gymnasium," roughly equivalent to a junior college in this country. Eventually, I would graduate with a combined major in biology and physics. At home I knitted with my sister Lone, and at school I sat knitting with classmates while professors lectured. At the start of the school year, I never stopped knitting to take notes, because I couldn't understand what was being said! Birgit, who had the palest hair and sunniest disposition I've ever known, befriended me. On breaks, she summarized the previous class in English and wrote down our assignments for the next day. At home, I penciled in English translations above every line

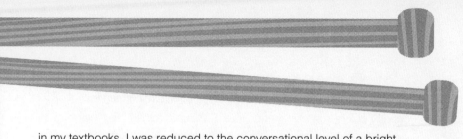

in my textbooks. I was reduced to the conversational level of a bright two-year-old. As a stranger without access to the intimacy of adult conversation, I often took solitary walks to our rocky shoreline. The endless expanse of cold water stretched out from the fjord into the North Sea and reflected my deep sense of isolation. By Christmas I would have developed a comfortable fluency in Danish, but in the meantime, Birgit and Lone sat with me as I silently knitted forward.

Campus clicks along
*   Without hurry or dawdle*
No sweater exams!

Island Traditions

In Denmark, most knitters I saw were female, though I saw a few men knitting in town. It hadn't been that long ago that fishermen in that country of five hundred islands had developed and knitted their own sweaters. I fell in love with that style, the feel of the smooth but slightly knobby wool in a tightly woven pattern intended to resist fierce winds and chilly water. I knitted one for my boyfriend in navy, the traditional color that conveniently matched his eyes. In my class at the gymnasium, only Ole and Drewsen knit with the girls. All they knit were hats in Fair Isle patterns.

The Practice Is the Point

I know of a male knitter who calls his stitches "hearts and bumps"—hearts for the knits and bumps for the purls. Compared to my early days of perfectionistic knitting, I now live a more placid practice. It is no longer about forcing the work and enduring it. Life is ever pregnant with herself, I am ever becoming, and endpoint is not the point. This sweater I knit may not become a sweater. I've decided goals must pleasure and motivate me, not drive me into walls. I remind myself that many goals exist to be relinquished, like seeds not meant to germinate. My knitting builds faith in this. I sit to play and question the one stitch. Oh, and then the next. All the unpredictable endpoints come in their own time. My hearts and bumps, they lead me.

Call It Evolution

Unlike some Danes I knew, I never learned to identify size of needles by sight. I did learn to use double points and adapt patterns. I became conversant with varieties of yarn, their textures and weights. Friends taught me different ways of casting on and a way to invisibly cast off. Scandinavians traditionally knit in multiple colors, like a brocade, weaving in the contrasts with complicated stitch patterns and tiny needles. They inspired me to tackle complex projects, and I succeeded wondrously. It was my rabid knitting era. Out of that tenure, I could grow into the relaxed, come-what-may knitter I am today.

Wide Open

Recently our council on aging interviewed people older than ninety and published a series in our local newspaper. As a young woman, ninety-nine-year-old Elizabeth Meyers moved to this country from Denmark. (I bet she knows how to knit!) When interviewed, she said, "The best thing about getting older is that you don't care. And when I say I don't care it doesn't mean I don't care unhappily. But that I don't care happily." I may never evolve as much as Elizabeth, but in moments when I knit, I'm grateful to taste the joy she describes—"I don't care happily."

Quietly gauging
Fingering the fabric fit
Laughing the inches

Count-to-ten Stitches

My husband Calvin and I were twenty-two years old when we married in 1974. His mother and I matched in height and weight, had similar features and coloring, and shared the same birthday. We were both anxious perfectionists, which meant we were often bossy and critical. Author and psychologist Harville Hendrix says people attract mates who in some way reflect back childhood wounds. This provides grist for couples to help each other heal and mature. They can consciously support one another to abandon childhood resentments and become more fully functioning adults. My husband appreciates and loves his mother, Ivah, but he also had his early struggles with her. Initially, I found Ivah a strong woman worthy of filling in as the mother figure I'd been seeking. I couldn't believe she cooked such wonderful meals and sent us home with cookies. I shushed my husband whenever he disagreed with or resisted his mother's directives. When we visited, she insisted we attend her church. Because she found my outfits lacking, I agreed to wear Ivah's clothes (including a slip, hose, and string of pearls!). As years passed, I grew less accommodating, and Ivah and I developed a peer relationship. No doubt, we two strong-willed women still find times when we irk one another. This is where the magic of knitting serves me once again. While Ivah talks, I knit in pleasure, with detached ease. The knitting becomes like a focal point used during labor, on a less dramatic scale. For the past few years, my husband and I have escaped the doldrums of February by spending a week at an eco-tourist resort on the Yucatan Peninsula in Mexico. Last year I told Ivah we would be returning there for the fourth time. "Oh," she said and lifted her chin, "that's the place where people eat with their feet sticking in the sand!" I nodded, smiled, and kept knitting.

When the day wearies
  Good company with knitting:
Honey and olives

Matching Insides with Outsides

Early childhood curriculums could include knitting as a self-soothing skill. I know knitting helps me stay easy with my own inside feelings, regardless of my surroundings. I've lost count of the many venues in which I have knit in order to ease myself, but they've included classrooms, medical waiting rooms, airports, courtrooms, public meetings, and peer support groups. Once I knitted during an Atlanta Hawks basketball game I attended with my sons and husband. They laughed, not in a mean-spirited way. The game bored me, but I was happy to sit with them while I knitted.

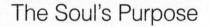

The Soul's Purpose

In the fall of my first year at law school in Chapel Hill, North Carolina, I was ambivalent and terrified. At that point in my life I really knew little about being, only doing. I had not yet heard Joseph Campbell's "follow your bliss" adage, nor run across Carl Jung's concept of the "soul's purpose." Those would have terrified me as well. Women comprised three percent of our law school population, which was consistent with national averages in 1974. Among other reasons, I consciously knew I was becoming a lawyer to prove the value of women in our culture, specifically to my father, and for my mother's sake. The young feminist Gloria Steinem spoke on campus that semester. When she called for questions, one cocky young man stood and asked if she was a lesbian. She answered, "Are you my alternative?" Law school was a painful ordeal. In my mind, many of the professors were simply sadists who falsely justified humiliating us in class, saying it was necessary to prepare us for courtroom work. My study carrel, my haven, was sequestered in a windowless room with blinking fluorescent lights. The first day there I carefully hand-printed and tacked on the tag board a quote from Gandhi: "The means are more important than the ends." I didn't dare draw attention to myself by knitting in class, but I stashed in my

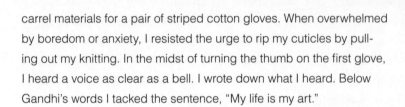

carrel materials for a pair of striped cotton gloves. When overwhelmed by boredom or anxiety, I resisted the urge to rip my cuticles by pulling out my knitting. In the midst of turning the thumb on the first glove, I heard a voice as clear as a bell. I wrote down what I heard. Below Gandhi's words I tacked the sentence, "My life is my art."

Small angle of ear
The skull breathing confusion
Knitting and listening

Remembering How Good Life Can Be

In the fall of 1974 I was newly married and sick. For several weeks I crawled in and out of bed with a severe and rare type of kidney infection. Nights heralded fever spikes and wracking pain. Through my bedroom window, a stunning view of fall color provided a pittance of pleasure. One evening, when I thought I was crying silently, my young husband rolled over. "Honey, are you okay?" Words popped out in a voice I didn't recognize. "I just want to knit."

The next day my former college roommate and knitting buddy Betsy brought me two skeins of variegated wool that mimicked the colors of leaves on our trees. I pulled size 7 circular needles from my collection, cast on a comfortable number of stitches, and started an unscripted project. My mind was dense and heavy as a wet log in the forest, but my fingers knew the way. From the ashes of that illness came my favorite winter hat, one I still wear more than three decades later.

My Giant Grasshopper

Early in my first pregnancy, I dreamed my baby's birth and gender. "He" was eight pounds. He was healthy. I held him in my arms, ecstatic. No one was comfortable looking at him except me. I wasn't concerned. I looked baby Zachary in his eyes and said, "Yes, son, you are bright green. You're a grasshopper, and you're beautiful just the way you are."

In the winter of 1979 my husband and I lived in the high mountains of rural southwest Virginia. My neighbor Wilma, who had borne her eight children at home, put her hands on my belly and confirmed the baby was a boy. For my little elf I bought some silky finger-weight wool to knit a stocking cap with a tassel at the end. I picked a Fair Isle pattern to work in the round and chose palest blue as the dominant color. My inner imp picked two shades of pink to mix in with a darker blue and white.

At the hospital, the nurses raved about beautiful Zachary, but they raved even more about his cap. None of them had ever attempted knitting with multiple colors and wanted to know if it was terribly difficult. They turned the cap inside out and studied the different yarns carried on the back side. Zachary and I were happily escorted out of the hospital in a wheelchair. His stocking cap draped over my arm and protected his bald head from the cooler air outside.

Though I had chosen blue as the dominant color for Zach's cap, I was surprised while shopping to be told by strangers how beautiful my little girl was. Somehow, even flecks of pink on the head must have signaled "female." Though my husband has always been a gender liberal guy, this embarrassed him. He couldn't bring himself to take Zach out in public with that cap on his head. For my part, I loved explaining that Zachary was a boy. And to tell the truth, he was "just as pretty as a girl."

All boys made of this
Warm and soft and so, so sweet
Knit them into pink

Is It a Boy or a Girl?

I've ignored television as an adult, but as a child, my favorite show was the comedy series *I Love Lucy*. The Lucille Ball character reminded me of my mother, a wild and creative woman. Lucy's expansive ideas and tenacious boldness always got her into trouble, but that never stopped her. When Lucy was actually pregnant with her second child, later known as "little Ricky," she knit on her show. I believe it was a sweater and a cap for the baby. She didn't know the sex at that point. No color was ever mentioned, and since the show was filmed in black and white, what Lucy held in her hands simply looked pale. She could have been knitting in any color, but my bet would be pastel blue, pink, or that safe yellow from the fifties. I think the bolder colors we can now use for babies makes the knitting much more fun. I bet Lucy would agree.

Nursing Dad

"The real poems are written in the heart's blood," writes poet Joseph Stroud. When my second son, Isaac, was three months at my breast, I was thirty years old, on maternity leave, and spending one day a week with my fifty-three-year-old father. He was dying of metastatic melanoma. Every Tuesday morning my mother ran out the door as I walked in with Isaac in my arms. Over my shoulder hung one bag filled with diapers and knitting. I spent my time knitting socks and nursing—nursing Isaac and nursing Dad. Nursing Dad meant silently sitting by him while he lay on the den sofa. When he asked, I jumped up to bring water, tissues, a blanket, or some small portion of food or drink that he would lay aside once I fetched it.

Given Dad's personal history, he had often been cruel and abusive. But along the way, I can also say he gifted me with crucial moments of nurturing and wisdom. My heart yearned for some easing of his dying process, for him and my mother, but they wouldn't ask for any help. Even if a hospice had existed in our small North Carolina town, I doubt they would have used it. The word "death" was not being spoken.

For my own heart, I yearned for a peacemaking with my dad before he died, any smidgeon of authentic connection. One day I broke the silence. "Dad, if I were you, I think I would be really angry about what's going on."

"I'm not angry!" he said sharply. I looked back at the argyle socks I was knitting for his cold feet. A few minutes passed before he reconsidered.

"I'm not angry," he said. "But I am disappointed. I'm disappointed I won't get to see Isaac grow up." Had it been possible between us, I would have cried openly. I would have touched my dad with gentle caution, because everywhere on his body hurt. Instead, I poured my heart's blood into stitching his socks, warm brown socks that matched his eyes. He would never get to wear them.

Sitting through each hour
Dark amber of my knitting
Linking love with grief

Heart Strings

In his book *The Heart's Code*, Paul Pearsall says the heart thinks and feels, and that its cells remember our lives. He recounts stories of heart transplant patients who go through periods of having memories and traits of the person who donated the new heart. Some scientists believe the heart, not the brain, is our truest seat of intelligence. From an electromagnetic standpoint, the heart is five thousand times more powerful than the brain. No wonder when I knit for someone else, I feel centered in my heart.

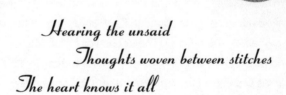

Hearing the unsaid
    Thoughts woven between stitches
The heart knows it all

Being Loved

What I most remember about my mother's large, extended family is their eyes. As early as preschool I began giggling with my siblings, calling those relatives "the red-eyes" behind their backs. I never heard anyone mention "alcoholism" or even use the euphemism "a drinking problem." Three years after my father's death, my siblings and I sat in a windowless room with my fifty-three-year-old mother and our counselor. For the six weeks prior, everyone but Mom had been meeting to train for an alcoholism intervention. We had our prepared notes. We individually went around the circle and told Mom we loved her and asked her to go into treatment. Each time, without hesitation and with indignation, she refused. The counselor pulled a flip-chart forward and angled it in Mom's direction. As the woman sketched and labeled circles within circles, she talked about the antecedents of alcoholism, the genetic propensities, and the layers of defenses against its core of pain. In a last attempt to push Mom toward a choice for treatment, the counselor said, "Frances, alcoholism destroys relationships and blocks love." Mom was silent for a moment. Then she responded in a

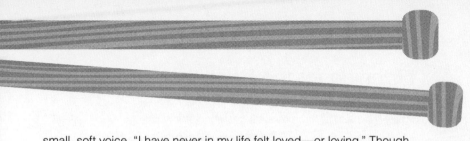

small, soft voice. "I have never in my life felt loved—or loving." Though that statement is too absolute for me, it was the truest, saddest thing I ever heard her say. Now, when I think back on that day, I wonder why I never knit something beautiful for my mother.

Years with words and yarn
Hunger older than speaking
Twisting wistfulness

Listening for the Beat

I have read that at three months gestation, every little girl baby has all her egg gametes fully formed and stored in her ovaries. This would mean the egg part of me nested inside my mother for six months as she floated in the warm salt bath of my grandmother's womb. The three of us snuggled as one. Only nineteen years later, as an embryo afloat in my mother's womb, I must have thrilled to the blood whooshing pace of her unique heartbeat. Today, my less keen ears are sometimes stressed and confused by the erratic mix of daily cadences. When I feel the call to focus on a single beat again, I pick up my metal needles. They act as small clapping bells, ringing me into prayerful ease. I enter their steady rhythm. I become that steady rhythm.

Knitting with spirits—
Shedding again and again
What you think you know

"I'm still curious about one thing, Agnes. Why did you take up knitting?"

Agnes responded, "I read not long ago in the journal *Brain* that knitting increases the activity in the left pre-frontal cortex, causing less susceptibility to stress and a more positive attitude toward life. The article said meditation and trampoline jumping had similar neuro-logical benefits. I chose knitting because the outcome includes a scarf, a blanket, a sweater."

—from *No Ordinary Matter* by Jenny McPhee

Stitches That Danced

My son Zach was eight and his younger brother Isaac six when I took them in the mid-eighties to see *White Nights*. The movie's plot is secondary to the exquisite dance performances by both Gregory Hines and Mikhail Baryshnikov. Tears ran down my cheeks as I watched Gregory tap and Mikhail twirl. As the boys and I left the theater, we were clicking our heels. In the parking lot, they threw their hands up over their heads and sprang into the air. They left me behind, vaulting like Baryshnikov all the way to our small Toyota. At the back of the car, Zach made a final leap up onto the trunk, banked, turned, and hurled himself into the sky. His lengthy drop to the asphalt couldn't have been pleasant, but he jumped up laughing. After seeing that movie, Zach joined a modern dance class. At its conclusion, the kids performed a beautiful group recital at a public park in downtown Charlotte, North Carolina. Zach chose to wear buttermilk-colored sweat pants with an aqua sleeveless T-shirt, untucked. Around his neck he wore a silk scarf I'd knit, long and golden-flecked. He tied it so one end dangled to his knees. As he danced the circle with his friends, the scarf fluttered behind him. He told me he felt like a magician making gold in the air.

Enmeshed in my hands
Further than an eye can see
Innocent beauty

Beauty for Beauty's Sake

In her article "The Durable Hunger," author Doris Betts writes about the innate drive to create beauty for its own sake. She describes creatures living at the bottom of the ocean, vividly colored "in symmetrical markings that nothing else down there—blind in the dark—can see, designs that provide no disguise for enemies, no attraction for breeding, that send out no territorial messages or attractions for prey." When I knit, I am like that creature of the deep, unseen and living in beauty. As I stitch, the thirteenth-century Persian poet Rumi whispers in my ear: "Let the beauty we love be what we do."

Living in the Body

My family and I moved to Asheville, North Carolina, in the summer of 1989. Within the week, I found a job at a psychiatric hospital that included a unit for clients with substance abuse addictions. I'd left my job as a hospice director two years before to train as a massage therapist. Luckily for me, this hospital's medical director believed the journey to heal mind and spirit required direct attention to the body. Six months into my hospital practice, Gina dragged herself into my office looking down at the floor. When first admitted, she'd been given a diagnosis of multiple personality disorder. We had been working together for six weeks. Seated, with shoulders hunched and eyes still downcast, she spoke. "I have terrible news."

"What is it?"

"On top of everything else, now they tell me I'm schizophrenic."

I studied her carefully. "You don't look any different to me today than you did last week." She looked up and smiled. We laughed.

Gina always questioned me in detail about my knitting, which I did between sessions. Unfortunately, knitting was not an offered recreational activity. I assured her that finding knitting classes and groups would not be difficult once she left the hospital. A year later I sat knitting in my office, enjoying the view of snow-covered mountains. When a knock came on my door, I thought my next client was early. Instead, it was Gina, who had gotten permission to enter the locked ward for a quick visit with me.

"Look!" She held out her mittened hands, and then twirled the scarf at her neck. Finally, she patted the hat on her head as she turned in a circle. "I knit all this!"

"Wow!" I said. She had knit all three in matching stripes of orange, purple, and green. "Yeah," Gina grinned. "I came to thank you. You taught me how to live in my body, and that was a doorway out of hell. Now, knitting helps me stay here." She patted her heart. "I can't explain it."

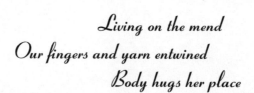

Living on the mend
Our fingers and yarn entwined
Body hugs her place

A Knitting Century (Almost)

My friend Gail is an incredible weaver, has a textile design degree, and teaches all levels of knitters. She tells beginners one of the biggest boons of knitting is how it helps a person stay centered and focused. Gail's ninety-six-year-old mother has been a knitter all her life. Now nearly blind, she still knits. Gail helps her with little problems like dropped stitches. Her mother likes to listen to books on tape, but had the problem of falling asleep and losing her place in the story. Because "she falls asleep when she knits," Gail suggested her mother knit while she listened to her tapes. This proved a big success. Her mother completed a large poncho by the time she finished two books on tape.

Broken Dreams

It was spring 1992 in the mountains of North Carolina. I was forty years old. My friend Mary was sick with cancer. After she lost all her hair to chemo, I decided to shave my head. I stood in the bathroom with my husband's razor and clippers in my hand. My nine-year-old son Isaac called to me through the door. I told him to wait. Hair fell and filled the wastebasket. Cool air brushed my newly bared skin. At last, with my handheld mirror, I proved myself bump and lump free.

Out in the hallway Isaac dragged me to the staircase where he could stand a step above. He grabbed my head with hot hands and positioned us for the best view. I felt him breathe against my scalp. "Wow, Mom. Amazing," he said. "I've never ever seen a bald woman's head this close!" I laughed. At the same time, I promised myself to knit two amazingly beautiful caps. Mary's would be in a blue to match her eyes.

Night full of crickets
Confusion and broken dreams
Skein of Russian blue

Sources of Yarn and Pleasure

A few days after shaving my head, I stopped for a lunch burrito at a fast-food chain. "Wow!" said the young man with dreadlocks who took my order. He seemed to have studied quite a lot about the symbolism of hair and no hair in humans. He told me Hindus shave their heads twice in a lifetime and offer up their shorn locks to the Divine. In Marele Day's novel *Lambs of God*, every spring after shearing their sheep three feral nuns shaved their own heads. Then they spun their hair into yarn combined with the sheep wool. I hadn't thought much about unusual sources of natural fibers until I read *Lambs of God*. I asked my fiber artist friend Gail what she knew about knitting with human hair. Turns out, like horsehair, it can be easily spun, but both end up prickly because of thick diameters and blunt ends. "Ever sit on a horsehair blanket or sofa, or wear a hair shirt? Really uncomfortable!" I don't spin, but Gail said it's best to mix a loved one's hair in with wool, and then line the garment after it is knit.

On the other hand, Gail raved about dog hair, and said it's a great fiber. "Only the combed undercoat of certain dogs can be used. Some of them, like Samoyeds or chows, have fiber as lovely as angora. Shepherds, golden retrievers, and mutts may also have a suitable undercoat. It is a quality of the individual dog, not just the breed." People also spin cat hair, but Gail wasn't familiar with that fiber.

I searched and found access to "dog yarn." I plan to knit a vest for my pet-sitting dog lover friend. And one day I want to try knitting with more plant fibers, like bamboo. What blessing that my knitting to-do list never shrinks, and the number of people I plan to knit for remains endless.

Knitting for others
The sacred ordinary
Dances in my hands

"While I knitted, I prayed to enter her grief;
I prayed light into every stitch; I prayed that she be comforted;
I prayed that she be healed."

–from *Knitting into the Mystery*
by Susan S. Jorgensen and Susan S. Izard

More Bad News

Mary came directly from her doctor's appointment to tell me she wasn't responding to treatments. We sat side by side on a worn loveseat in my sunroom and cried. Then we rubbed our heads together, which felt funny and made us laugh. "People must look at my bald head and think I'm a lesbian, a cancer patient, a Buddhist nun, or just a plum crazy woman," Mary said. "Of course, three out of four ain't bad."

We laughed again, and I pulled the soft cotton cap for Mary out of my knitting bag. "This feels good," she said when she put it on. She propped her feet up, laid back, and closed her eyes. I pulled out the other cap I was knitting for myself. A flock of robins appeared outside the open Florida windows, and I put my knitting down to watch them. They puffed up their orange-red breasts and kicked into an a cappella chorus. I'm sure it was the loudest racket I'd ever heard a group of songbirds make.

Mary stirred beside me. She sat up and smiled at the robins. "The birds must be happy with this day."

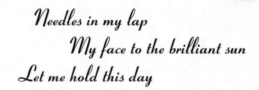

Needles in my lap
    My face to the brilliant sun
Let me hold this day

Timeless Time

Einstein theorized time as elastic. I agree. Sometimes I look up from my knitting, and an hour has passed in a minute. Sometimes, a minute passes in an hour. The gift is the same. In the moments my fingers speak with yarn, I live outside of time.

My Mother's Shawl

Mary died on a frigid day in January, the blue sky cloudless, and the sun so bright it cut like shards of glass. Family members would be coming into town for the funeral. Mom agreed I could offer her second home as a place for people to stay. But she said, "It's a mess." I could go clean up before the guests arrived.

Mom's two homes were not simply messy and unkempt. "Squalor" was the word used by a friend who spent the day scrubbing with me. When I removed sheets in one room, I found a shawl wedged behind the bed board against a wall. I pressed my face into the silky pink wool. When I smelled the shawl and inhaled the scent of my mother and her stale cigarettes, I instantly balled it up against my chest. Like a naughty child,

I left the house and hid my prize in the trunk of my car. My friend didn't witness this, and I doubt my mother ever missed the shawl.

I always admired my mother's flair. She was herself a thwarted artist, and she deeply appreciated the beauty of handmade things. Before I stored her shawl in the back of my closet, I examined it more closely. The label sewn at the neck named a local knitter. The shawl was large and simply designed with partly seamed sides that left armholes. When worn, it draped like an open coat.

In my life, I have not been a person who steals things, but after ten years, that shawl remains on the shelf in the back of my closet. I never wear it, but on certain occasions, I take it out, unwrap it, and hold it.

Faded cyclamen
Something knit and something lost
Fallen rose petals

"But even if all the experts didn't agree, I'd still know what knitting does for me . . . When I knit, as when I write, I find myself in ecstatic participation in a divinely animated world."

–from *Zen and the Art of Knitting*
by Bernadette Murphy

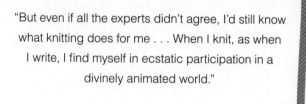

Losing a Mother

A week after the funeral, three friends and I arranged to celebrate Mary's life in a private ritual. I put on coat, mittens, and the cap I knitted for Mary the year before. I drove into the sunset taking in the beauty of that crisp January day. Suddenly, I was pulled from my reverie by a familiar scent. I sniffed and realized it was Mary! She was in the car with me. I heard her voice clearly say, "Most will lose their mothers in death. You must lose yours in life." I burst into tears.

Eight years later, in 1999, Mom and I were yelling on the phone. At some point I numbed out and fixated on an oddly misshapen spiderweb in the corner of the room. It looked as if the spider were ill. It was making jerky, erratic turns. The web it was attempting was not taking coherent form. Finally, the spider gave up. She dangled upside down by a thread. At the close of our conversation, Mom said she didn't care if I lived or died. She wanted no further connection with me. I asked that we not make it so absolute. At any time in the future, if either one of us felt called to contact the other, could we do so? She agreed to this, and we hung up. I never heard from her again. A year and a half later, Mom died at sixty-nine, the day before Mother's Day. Her heart, weakened by a lifetime use of alcohol and cigarettes, exploded. Earlier in the week I had felt an urge to contact her. As I did as a child, I made her a Mother's Day card. Instead of crayons, I used snippets of scrap yarn. With white glue I fashioned them into a strong oak tree covered with the many greens of spring leaves. Whatever I wrote in that card is lost to me, but I know it was very simple. I know I told her I loved her. I don't know if my mother read the card before she died.

Like mangled stitches
They come to me in sorrow
My mother's dark nights

A Talisman in Yarn

In *Women Who Run with the Wolves*, Clarissa Pinkola Estes says
Spider Woman, a goddess in some Native American cultures, "is in
charge of teaching the soul both protection and the love of beauty."
Spider Woman is a mother one woman I know carries inside herself.
Like the spider, this woman friend is a knitter. After she discovered
this inner mother, she designed and knit herself a black sweater. Spill-
ing over the chest is an enormous spider outlined in gold. It has a
deep blue thorax. The perfect brown buttons with dark centers are the
spider's piercing eyes. The sweater is really a vestment. My friend says
she often wears it for emotional comfort. When she needs to feel safe
and powerful, it really works.

Goodness and mercy:
    Many mothers knitting us
Held in steady arms

A Few Good Men

I was eight years old in 1959 when John F. Kennedy ran for president. That same year I learned to knit, and I read a biography of Eleanor Roosevelt, the wife of a president, and a great stateswoman in her own right. She was often photographed with her bulging knitting bag in hand. During the Kennedy campaign, what I most remember was the national clamor about his being a Roman Catholic, how that would lose him votes and possibly the election. This baffled me. Catholics were Christians. Kennedy was white. He was a man. I thought about my Jewish friend Anne Weisenberger. I thought about the black people I knew. I thought about myself, a girl who would one day become a woman. Inside me a voice promised, "When I grow up, a woman will be the president of the United States!"

After the century turned on January 1, 2000, I felt a surprising surge of sadness. Suddenly I flashed back to my childhood prediction and realized I would turn fifty with yet another white man ruling as president in the White House. Four years later, I take comfort in reading a recent poll that found 79 percent of Americans are comfortable with the idea of having a woman as president. This poll led me to other gender questions, like "Where are all the male knitters?" I'd seen a few

and I'd heard stories about them from other women knitters. I've found blogs on the Internet and support groups for "men who knit." In my own small life, however, at that point, I'd only known four male knitters. One of them was a psychotherapist, my age. His wife taught him to knit as a way to reduce stress.

Doc between sessions
Whipping out his knitting bag—
Knits to clear his mind

Macho Knitting

While searching the Internet I stumbled across an advertisement for "Men Who Knit" T-shirts and mugs. All were imprinted with a sweet-faced bulldog. One dictionary definition for bulldog is "a person known for courage or stubborn tenacity." In actual dog competitions, judging standards say the bulldog's chest must be "very broad, deep, and full." Its overall attitude should "suggest great stability, vigor, and strength." Was this mascot chosen to counter the still prevalent perception of male knitters as "sissies"? Perhaps "stubborn tenacity" is necessary for any man, gay or straight, to come out of the knitting closet.

Working at Home

Working as I do, alone at home, I sometimes find myself needing a whiff of humanity. I have a friend who likes to absorb its hustle and bustle by sitting and knitting at the mall. I prefer a sunny bench in the heart of our little city. Since Asheville, North Carolina, is a mountain tourist town, I get to watch a colorful stream of our own local people as well as global visitors walking by. The nice thing about knitting in an anonymous public place is people I don't know stop to ask questions about my work. It reminds me of my pregnancies, when strangers at the grocery store stopped to ask about my due date and future mothering plans. Actually, the conversations by my knitting bench are better. Questions about what I'm knitting, who it is for, and how long I've been at the craft soon lead to swapping snippets from our lives. Even an hour of this kind of knitting refills my half-empty glass. I'm able to return home with new vigor and enthusiasm for necessary tasks.

The shadow today
  A squirting sunshine in gray
Wise one sits to knit

Each in Her Own Way

I have learned early morning walks really are a boon to my spirits and overall health. A walking friend of mine actually knits as she goes. She wears a fanny pack filled with yarn on her belly and flips her stitches out in front of herself as she strides. I did try this once and failed miserably. It was like patting my head and rubbing my belly at the same time. I guess if I really wanted to, I could learn to do it. But in this case, I've decided to let knitting be knitting and walking be walking.

Knitting in Public

One of my childhood dreams was to become a ballerina. Instead, when my two sons were mostly grown, I convinced my husband to gift me with ballroom dance classes. We learned waltz, swing, polka, cha-cha, and others. Now my husband enjoys dancing more than I do. Evenings I don't want to go, I say, "Not tonight, Dear. I have a headache." The single women are always grateful.

In our town, all ages show up for ballroom dancing. Since more women than men usually attend, most women sit out a few dances. At one point, I decided to carry my knitting with me. In my bag was the half-finished decorative shawl for a young dancing friend's upcoming birthday. While others twirled on the floor, I nested happily by a table with silk-wool yarn gliding through my hands. The needles were size 5, plastic and pea green, a nice contrast to a fizzy red yarn.

My fingers fluttered to Frank Sinatra crooning "Strangers in the Night," and my vision fell to a soft blur. Then came the insistent tap on my shoulder. "Can you put that crochet down long enough to dance?"

"Sure," I said to Jim B., but took my time to settle the shawl-in-process. On the dance floor Jim led me in triple-step swing with what

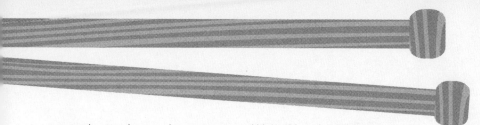

seemed extra vigorous loops, turns, and kicks. He ushered me back to my table and asked, "Now wasn't dancing with me more fun than that crochet?"

Later my knitter friend Betsy and I sat fondling my yarn and chatting. Jeffery L. interrupted to ask Betsy to dance. As she rose he leaned in to me. "Maria, from observing you, one would presume you enjoy knitting more than dancing." Betsy returned to our table and reported that she had set the record straight. She told Jeffery, "If Maria enjoyed knitting more than dancing, she would carry it out on the floor with you!"

Give the man a chance
        Stop knitting, put your shoes on,
Toss the shawl and dance!

The Sacred and the Profane

A couple of years ago my friend Jeanne and I were stranded for six hours at Newark Airport. We found refuge in the "Meditation Center," which shook but mostly muffled the airport noise. In the windowless room three short rows of plastic chairs faced a podium lit with dim lights. At an odd angle to the corner in the back lay a small rug with tones of red and gold. Beside it a sign read, "No shoes beyond this point." We had woken early, and Jeanne had taken a Dramamine prior to our flight cancellation. She draped herself across three chairs and fell asleep. I sat a row down and pulled out my knitting. In the middle of timeless time, the door behind me swished open. I heard shuffling and whispering. Leaning forward as if in prayer, I sneaked a peek under one armpit. Two men by the Persian rug were removing their shoes. I sat back to knit, and they began chanting.

With another quick peek, I saw the men kneeling side by side, folding forward on bent knees as they repeated, at least in part, what sounded like "Allah," or more acoustically apparent to my ear, "Uuuuh—LAHHH-HHHHHHH." At the end of each "Allah" their foreheads touched the rug. As they rose up their voices careened to a higher, indecipherable pitch. I assumed they were Muslims facing Mecca.

That holy wash of one of God's many names anointed me while I knit. I breathed easily and savored those sacred moments, until, like a train roaring down the tracks, Jeanne blasted forth with snoring honks. I couldn't reach to shake her, and I struggled not to profane the praying by bursting into laughter. In desperation, I stabbed the metal number 3 knitting needle into my left thumb—perhaps the only time in my life I've ever used a knitting needle to inflict pain.

Jeanne never stopped snoring. I woke her after the men left. On our way out, for the first time I noticed a sign by the door: "Please do not EAT, DRINK, or SLEEP in this room."

To knit here right now
Waiting is no disaster
Gentle round and round

KNIT ONE, HAIKU TOO

Yarn to Ashes

Just a few years ago, my friend Becky's house burned to the ground. The first week she spent in total shock and confusion. Didn't go to work. Didn't make meals. Didn't kiss her husband. The second week she began knitting—all day, every day. With donated scraps of yarn from friends, she cast thirty stitches onto size 10 needles and knit in continuous garter stitch. Two weeks after that, she stopped. She meticulously stacked wood by the wreckage of her former home and placed her motley knit piece curled on top. She invited friends to a ritual bonfire. A potter gave her a green glazed ceramic box with a lid. In it Becky mixed ashes from the bonfire with ashes from the leavings of her old home. Her filled box sits on the mantel of a new fireplace in her new home. In moments of deep sadness, Becky pauses by the box and brushes her fingers across the cool porcelain lid.

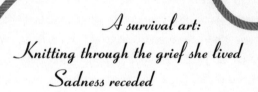

A survival art:
Knitting through the grief she lived
Sadness receded

KNIT ONE, HAIKU TOO

107

In Sickness and in Health

Beginning at age forty-five, and through the next eight years, I suffered bouts of what I came to call "digestive distress." Sometimes these lasted only a few days, sometimes for months, and my life altered radically. I stopped working a scheduled day job, cut back on all my activities, and began writing at home. This way I could better manage my times of incapacity without as much disappointment and disruption to my life.

Over the years, sophisticated tests and scans found nothing wrong with my insides. One doctor offered the label "abdominal migraine." Often I reverted to eating only baby food. I walked as much as possible and got massages. I spent hours in therapy and gleaned valuable insights. I bathed in the love of friends. This was all good, but nothing stopped the erratic attacks that clawed my days, my eating, and my sleep. I couldn't lie on my right side. I lived with a heating pad on my belly. I read. I wrote. I knit.

Just as I began writing this book, I fell deeply ill again. This episode began abruptly after eating a meal in the doldrums of March. I managed my pain as usual, but through the following six weeks, it worsened. The week prior to a scheduled beach vacation with friends, my new doctor said she wanted to check my gallbladder. I didn't want to cancel the vacation with husband and friends. My doctor scheduled tests for the week I would return. I left town with a prescription bottle of pain pills and a knitting project in hand. I would knit a birthday scarf for my friend Ting in Minnesota. "Ting" means "graceful" in Chinese. I selected muted colors of gold, red, and purple. I chose light silk and wool blend for the sweet caress on my fingers. To make it easy, I would knit connected garter stitch squares on size 4 needles. At each end I would knit ruffles with variegated yarn that would complement the solid colors and add a little pizzazz. Ting's birthday would arrive the last week of May. I needed to start and finish the present during my vacation. And, purely for myself, I wanted a way to surround my current pain with beauty and peace.

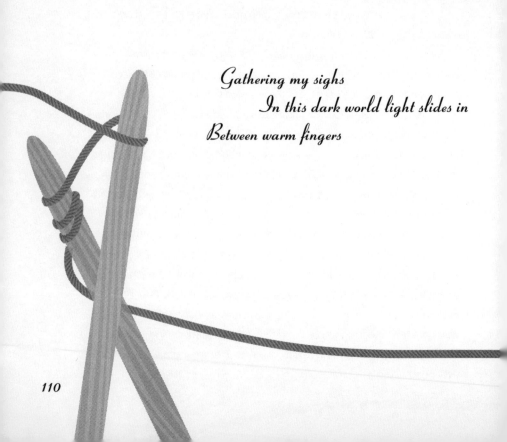

Gathering my sighs
 In this dark world light slides in
Between warm fingers

"Since the invisible world is far greater than anything we can manage to experience in this physical realm, it's nice to have a hobby, habit, or practice that can bring us into a stillpoint within, a place each of us must find within ourselves—in our own unique way."

—from *The Zen Commandments* by Dean Sluyter

A Lost Needle

Six of us arrived Saturday afternoon to vacation in a front row house on Folly Beach, an island town, and the closest beach to Charleston, South Carolina. I knew once settled in, we wouldn't leave. It was too easy and too pleasant to walk to Bert's little grocery store, the pier, and any of the various diners.

That evening, I settled on the sofa with my heating pad and birthday scarf project. Everyone else played a fast action card game our friend Ginger learned from her Louisiana grandmother. I got up and down to make cups of herbal tea with the small hope of eliminating my abdominal pain.

The house was quiet on Sunday morning when I woke to a clear sky and numinous sunrise. I slipped out of bed planning to sit, knit, and watch in solitude. But the free needle was not skewered in my yarn. Everyone scoured the house. My husband and his friend turned the sofa upside down and stuck their hands deep into its batting. Though I wanted to finish the scarf that week, I was reluctant to drive off island for new needles.

On a walk after lunch, Ginger and I paused marsh-side at a yard sale. The woman who lived there told me she wanted ten dollars for a set of silver plate flatware that belonged to her grandmother. I had to buy it for the iced teaspoons alone. The previous year, without consulting my husband, I'd given ours away, wrongly thinking "we" never used them.

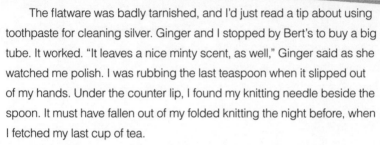

The flatware was badly tarnished, and I'd just read a tip about using toothpaste for cleaning silver. Ginger and I stopped by Bert's to buy a big tube. It worked. "It leaves a nice minty scent, as well," Ginger said as she watched me polish. I was rubbing the last teaspoon when it slipped out of my hands. Under the counter lip, I found my knitting needle beside the spoon. It must have fallen out of my folded knitting the night before, when I fetched my last cup of tea.

With needle back in hand, I did finish Ting's scarf by the end of the week.

By misty streetlights
Early morning knitting time
The kettle whistles

All Shall Be Well

Visual artist Robert Henri wrote, "Do not let the fact that things are not made for you, that conditions are not as they should be, stop you. Go on anyway. Everything depends on those who go on anyway." Sometimes "going on anyway" means stopping the struggle to hold on to a presupposed plan. Sometimes I can wait when stymied, like a child at ease, and watch for possibility. Often out of this waiting, something blossoms forth to set a better fruit than I ever knew existed.

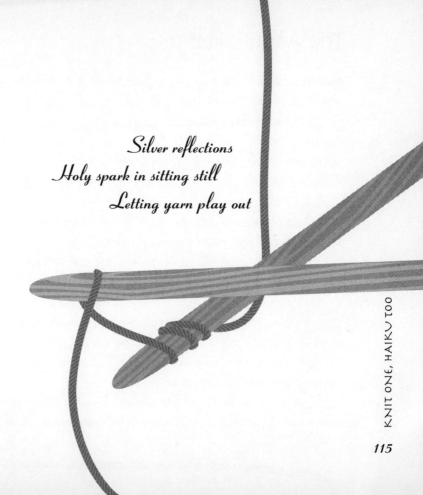

Silver reflections
Holy spark in sitting still
Letting yarn play out

The Angel's Hand

Back home in Asheville, I went through tests that revealed a compromised gallbladder. That pear-shaped organ tucked under my liver was not holding and titrating bile properly. This is a less common malady than blockage with stones or sludge. Unfortunately, that malfunction had not been investigated during my years of chronic illness. Fortunately, however, surgery would be performed the second day of June.

My consummate knitter friend Elizabeth often prepares people for medical procedures. She listens to individual fears and hopes and from them creates recorded suggestions for the subconscious. Twice a day for five days prior to surgery I listened to Elizabeth's reassuring voice on my personalized tape.

My surgeon was very large. She looked like an eager young teenager with long blond hair. I saw her as an alpine maiden, a strong, capable woman who could milk cows in the evening while singing, "The hills are alive with the sound of music . . . ," and then go home at night to knit socks by candlelight.

My surgical process proceeded without a hitch. I was prepped, given a memory-blocking drug, kissed by my husband, and rolled into the procedure room. Lying on my back in the low light, I heard soft rustling preparations around me. My arms were strapped down. A tall, luminous figure suddenly appeared above me by my left side. For a moment her warm hand covered mine entirely, and then squeezed gently before letting go. The mask floated down over my face. I went under in total peace.

At some point my surgeon ducked into the recovery room to tell me I had "a beautiful anatomy," but my removed gallbladder had been very scarred and adhered, indicating numerous attacks throughout the years. "Thank you so much for holding my hand before surgery," I said, so grateful for the energy of the prayer I had felt.

My alpine angel looked startled. "No one ever remembers that!" I did, despite memory-suppressing drugs. And I hope I never forget that feeling of a larger reality touching me.

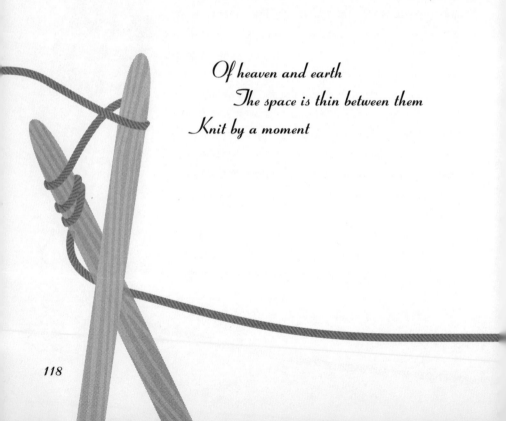

Of heaven and earth
The space is thin between them
Knit by a moment

"The web of our life is of mingled yarn, good and ill together."

—William Shakespeare,
All's Well That Ends Well

Praying and knitting
Covers those you love with love
Disguised as a shawl

Love from Betsy

In June our southern mountains gift us with warm days, usually in the high 70s, but I had lost more than twenty pounds prior to and following surgery. I felt icy to the marrow of my bones. Betsy, a public health nurse who works with Hispanic moms and their children, decided to knit her first prayer shawl for me. On the Internet she found Susan S. Jorgensen and Susan S. Izard's instructions (*Knitting into the Mystery*).

When she brought me the shawl, Betsy apologized. She explained that the yarn was really too thick. Also, she was disappointed in its texture, not soft, silky, and light for summer wear, but coarse, nubby, and maybe too warm to use in the heat. I thanked her for the fire engine red color she knows I favor, and I assured her I was in need of deep heating.

Since I had sunk into the cold waters of my frightened five-year-old self, I could hardly swim. Words failed me for the first time in my adult life. I could not read, much less write. I seemed untethered, but tethered enough to feel new pains of postsurgical healing, along with its different kind of digestive distress.

Fondling Betsy's prayer shawl, I found it would not park on my shoulders. Some wordless part of me desired wrapping and pinning it securely around my midsection. Though I had two knitting projects waiting, I couldn't read their instructions. Swaddled in my shawl, I sat on my screen porch and listened to our squadron of songbirds. When I could, I lifted a hank from the basket beside me to slowly wind it into a ball.

A hesitation—
Pool of yarn in which I found
Nowhere to somewhere

Things I Cannot Change

I think poet and memoirist May Sarton once wrote that the hardest thing in life is to be aware of suffering, suffering about which we can do nothing. It is a human challenge to face powerlessness over certain pain, whether it belongs to us or someone else. In his book *Dark Nights of the Soul*, Thomas Moore advocates practicing an appreciation for the dark periods of our lives. He suggests, "If you feel lost, be lost in ways that suit you and make you feel like a participant in your life." Some weeks after gallbladder surgery, when I couldn't see myself improving, when not much was visibly happening in my life, I was able to crawl into the quiet motion of knitting.

Monkey See . . .

My neighbor Alice kept good watch over me after my surgery. She saw me not knitting, scoured the library and brought me a book of knit animals to be made mostly in garter stitch pieces, seamed, and stuffed. I had no specific child in mind, but I was drawn to a funny little monkey similar to old-style sock monkeys seen in stores. I wasn't ready to do any kind of shopping yet, so I searched the house and found a forgotten cone of golden brown sport-weight chenille yarn to use for most of the body. Next I located an off-white skein of worsted-weight wool I would use for the face, hands, feet, and inside of the ears. I didn't bother gauging. Size and quality control were of no concern. Whatever this creature became or not, it would emerge out of the wordless life I was leading.

Unimpressive brown rectangles knit up fairly easily to form arms, legs, trunk, and tail. The face, hands, feet, and inner ears were more of a challenge. When they seemed not to be uniformly working, I pushed and shoved errant stitches into place. I figured I could seam out some of the imperfections.

When I finished and stuffed the basic monkey, I stitched on a mouth and nose with brown embroidery floss. In a button box I found two coconut shell buttons perfect for the eyes. With every visit, my twenty-three–year-old son Isaac said, "I want this monkey." I promised it to him, but told him I needed to admire it awhile.

When my older friend Patte dropped by to visit, she said, "You are not giving this monkey to anyone!" I thought about my strange reluctance to give it to Isaac each time he asked. I thought about not having stuffed animals as a child and not liking dolls. As odd as it seemed to me, I truly wanted this monkey for myself.

A month passed and I was reading again. I looked up "monkey" in my world symbols book. In China, the monkey is a symbol for "transformation."

Glittering nothing
　　How knitting carries me through
Stream of sympathy

"After all, the important thing is not so much what you knit as what happens while you knit it. Where the interior journey takes you. What you find there. How you are transformed when you come back home."

—from *The Knitting Sutra*
by Susan Gordon Lydon

Breathe in and exhale
Go with——let go——stitch again
　　Rhythm in chaos

Winds of the Canyon

Only in brief moments did I both live in and transcend the nitty-gritty of my surgical recovery. During deeply painful times, keeping faith in life demands much tenacity, deep soul-searching, and a bag of tricks—both old and new. In the years I spent volunteering and then creating and directing a hospice, I became an Elisabeth Kübler-Ross groupie. I followed her as much as possible on her speaking circuit. She inspired me to honor my darker emotions, as well as my wounds and scars. She always said the winds of the canyon had carved her unique features, and she wouldn't have had it any other way.

Pain can cancel out joy. Some religions say this journey into the void is one way to meet God. Buddhists speak of resting in empty space. Three days after my operation I had a dream. I am about to begin a bicycle race. The shot goes off, but everyone leaves me behind as I struggle to get my feet into toe clips on the pedals. When I look up, the cycling specks disappear on the horizon, and I realize I am out of the race. Around me in all directions, there is nothing but glinting sand and blue sky. I am standing alone on a high, endless plain. I feel relieved. No point in striving to catch up. My dream and the amoeba-time that followed it helped me shed fears of the unoccupied moment. Through

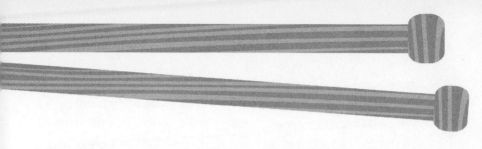

many knitting weeks I pondered the vast, incomprehensible open space of minute atoms. Sometimes I stopped my knitting and lifted it to my face. I stretched the woven yarn apart and peered through many tiny holes. I saw myself alive in a world on either side of the fabric. I felt stitches made of the spaces in-between.

Affirming this life
A way in and a way out
My thread loops forward

Confessions of Fear

I have heard that the best cure for a broken story is another story. Through some years I followed Christopher Reeves's heroic journey after he fell from his horse and became a quadriplegic. Just before he died he wrote an article about fear that acknowledged the despair he and his wife had felt. "Did we feel uplifted by this challenge? Absolutely not." Like Reeves, for me, fearlessness no longer holds the dictionary definition of "living without fear." In fact, I don't even aspire to that supposed virtue. Instead, I believe I'm asked to honestly acknowledge any fear that pops up. Then by grace, I can make clearer choices for transmuting fear into my most joyful destiny.

Jik Jik Jik

Maxine Hong Kingston's Chinese mother taught her a "Woman Warrior chant" she fully translates in *The Fifth Book of Peace*. "Jik jik jik. Jik jik jik," is the first line of that chant. "Jik" means "to weave," "to knit," "to heal." When my concentrating mind left me the summer after gallbladder surgery, I was reduced to primitive panic. I constantly flipped back into the dangerous house of my childhood. Even my wonderful home with my husband was no longer a house of safe haven. I was being asked to summon up my own "woman warrior," to surrender to my terror, but not collapse into it. I discovered a safe liminal space on our screened porch. I spent as much time there as possible. It reminded me of happy moments spent rocking and knitting beside my grandfather Sug on his screened porch. In a magical way, the porch seemed free of the darkness that had invaded my house and protected me from the unknown and too bright that lived outside its boundaries. The old self-loather in me rose up to shame my "weakness." I brought knitting projects to the porch and left them there. As I knit through my days, my "woman warrior" grew stronger, though I wasn't always aware of it at the time. I remember a pregnant young woman in a novel overwhelmed by her husband's death sat knitting an entire winter by

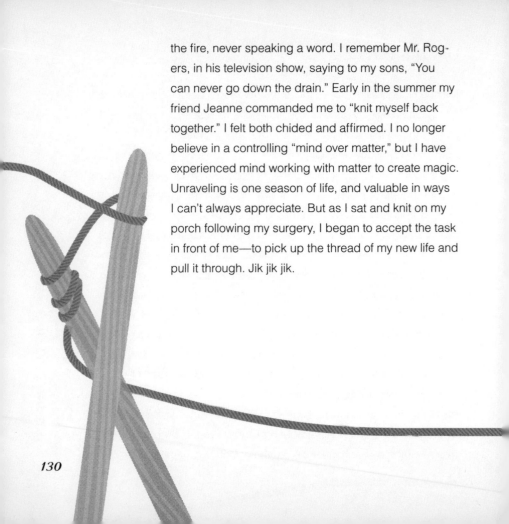

the fire, never speaking a word. I remember Mr. Rogers, in his television show, saying to my sons, "You can never go down the drain." Early in the summer my friend Jeanne commanded me to "knit myself back together." I felt both chided and affirmed. I no longer believe in a controlling "mind over matter," but I have experienced mind working with matter to create magic. Unraveling is one season of life, and valuable in ways I can't always appreciate. But as I sat and knit on my porch following my surgery, I began to accept the task in front of me—to pick up the thread of my new life and pull it through. Jik jik jik.

How to trust the dark
        The mind seeks and falls apart
Little thread that winds

Greater Than

"The mind is what the brain does," wrote James Shreve in *National Geographic* magazine. Scientists still cannot explain why human consciousness exceeds the physical boundaries of our brains. We intuit the mystery by the way we describe experience. "My head is spinning" means our brain isn't thinking clearly. "You break my heart" speaks of the love sheltered there. "It makes me sick to my stomach" may indicate fear or disgust rumbling in the gut. What about the hands? Touching is what the hands do. And through the items she makes, a knitter is doubly blessed to touch others with both love and beauty.

Healthy Selfishness

Poet Ed Hirsch says poets are "makers." They draw invisible words from the air and make them into poems. In my mind, hands are the penultimate symbol for making. How wondrous that through gestures of my hands and words I may serve others. I confess, however, that as both a knitter and a poet, I do my making to please me first!

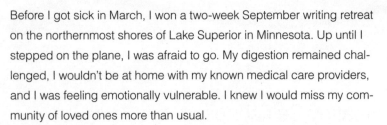

Nurse Whatley

Before I got sick in March, I won a two-week September writing retreat on the northernmost shores of Lake Superior in Minnesota. Up until I stepped on the plane, I was afraid to go. My digestion remained challenged, I wouldn't be at home with my known medical care providers, and I was feeling emotionally vulnerable. I knew I would miss my community of loved ones more than usual.

In preparation for the journey, I resisted setting up and learning what might be involved with the use of a laptop. I called Carlton Whatley to prime the little machine and tutor me in its usage. Carlton is an unusual man who spent seventeen years as a hospital nurse before he switched fields. He understands the ailments of my body and my computer and gives sound advice about them both. I should pay him double!

Though not exactly a technophobe, I find when things go wrong with an electronic writing tool, my vagus nerves fire wildly and make my stomach jump. I become a deer in the headlights. Despite the use of deep-breathing, self-talk, or other self-soothing tools, this nerve response seems beyond conscious control. Carlton is very sympathetic. He knows a lot about the vagus nerves, which feed the abdomen and are the two longest cranial nerves in the body.

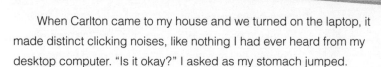

When Carlton came to my house and we turned on the laptop, it made distinct clicking noises, like nothing I had ever heard from my desktop computer. "Is it okay?" I asked as my stomach jumped.

Carlton smiled serenely and patted my back. "It's fine."

Okay, I told myself, time to reframe. This little laptop buddy is my clicking wizard. He's like the cricket on the hearth, a sign of good luck and fortune. When I am writing and hear his click, I will remember the sound of my needles as I knit. Thank goodness for one vocation that requires only two sticks and some string.

Mind's cacophony
Jabbering technology
Yes, my yarn calms me

All Thumbs

The opposable thumb is an amazing feature of our human anatomy. Humans have become adept makers because of it. I recently read that one cup of broccoli has enough folate to grow a brand new thumb. Since I'm not a starfish, I know I can never regrow my thumbs, but I did wonder if I could knit without them. I knelt by the couch, wedged needles through my fingers, and threaded yarn with my teeth. Slowly and arduously, three twisted stitches introduced themselves. Now I knit with a larger gratitude for what thumbs make possible.

Thumbing through this wool
A numinous journeying
Reverence for life

Who Is My Copilot?

Coming home from the writing retreat on Lake Superior I waited five hours for the one direct evening flight from Minneapolis to Asheville. At the designated departure time, an attendant behind the desk announced, "Folks, we're all set and ready to go—but we can't find our copilot." As one angry swarm, passengers rose to demand their complaint forms.

While people furiously scribbled on the paper in their laps, I wrestled a stressful knitting project, a trendy scarf for my son's girlfriend. The tinsel yarn hurt my fingers and the hateful size 17 plastic needles looked like ballpoint pens for first graders. What in the world could have happened to our copilot who had not even called in? Deathly illness? A wreck? Was she or he okay? Fifteen minutes passed and the young woman behind the desk announced we would snag a copilot from another flight arriving any minute now. I lay my knitting aside and approached the desk. The attendant waited with a plastered smile. "No complaint form for me," I said. "What I need is your reassurance. Will this new copilot be fully rested?"

"Oh, yes, ma'am." Her smile was bright. "FAA regulations are very strict. Only a certain number of in-air hours are allowed." Oh, no, like nurses, I thought. Impossible twelve hour shifts! We boarded the plane a half hour later and waited for our copilot to run across the airport. In the meantime, the captain announced, "Drinks are on the house." Loud cheering erupted. The woman beside me leaned in. "If they would hand out needles and yarn instead of drinks, maybe everyone could calm down." I looked over with envy at her baby sweater in progress. She let me stroke the fine yarn, and I sighed with relief. Just then a young man bounced onto the plane and flung his small bag into an upper compartment. "Are you our copilot?" I blurted out. "Yes, ma'am," he said with a cute salute. He looked perhaps sixteen, but very chipper, and surely adept with all things electronic and aeronautical.

Looking for Men Who Knit

This year I sought out Paul at Purl's Yarn Emporium, a local knit shop. Paul is a forestry student who works there part-time to support his "yarn habit." His mother taught him to knit at four years old when he was growing up in southern Indiana. As a younger man, he lived on the Outer Banks of North Carolina where he knotted fishing nets in his spare time and sold them to people in the local fishing industry. When he moved here to the mountains, he replaced knotting with knitting. "I had to have something to do with my hands."

I ask him why more guys don't knit.

"Unfortunately, our culture rigidly assigns activities based on gender," he says. "Too bad, because a lot of men are missing out." Paul is encouraged that more men of all ages seem to be coming into the store. "One guy is a house painter who grew up here. When he gets home, he knits. He's not interested in learning anything complicated. He knits only scarves because he just wants to relax."

I ask Paul if he thinks straight guys fear being pegged as gay if they become knitters. "Absolutely. But honestly, I'm thirty-one. I've been knitting for years, and no one has ever said or done anything to make me feel uncomfortable." He pauses. "You know, a lot of younger guys take up knitting today because it's supposed to make you a chick-magnet, but I don't think it ever helped me in that arena."

"Surely it has," I say. Paul has a girlfriend who studies microbiology and doesn't knit. "You knit for her, don't you? That's got to earn you brownie points." He grins. "Oh, sure!" he says with a sweet Midwestern twang.

His hands live in yarn
Feeding senses and the soul
Chick-magnet for sure!

Boys Will Be Boys

DiAnna is a church youth group leader who taught her charges to knit. She gave me names of high school senior boys willing to talk about their experiences. Reed said he enjoyed the tactile rewards of knitting and might take it up more seriously later in life when he isn't so busy. Willie, however, keeps knitting because it relaxes him. "It helps me unwind after a hard day at school. It gives my brain a rest." To keep it simple, he only knits scarves and then gifts people with them. Knitting wasn't modeled in Willie's family. In fact, his mother decided to learn the skill after he did. Five years into this new century, the Craft Yarn Council of America estimates that 4 to 5 percent of the knitting market is male. Reed and Willie believe the low numbers of male knitters are due to the "girlie stigma" still attached to guys who knit. But they also think this is rapidly changing. I thank them for forging the way for other guys.

Not a Family Legacy

My two grown sons had no interest in learning to knit when they were young boys and then teenagers living in my house. I, in turn, have never had the slightest interest in organized sports. However, my neighbor Alice is an avid baseball fan who closely follows professional league games. I perk up a little when she reports on the personal lives of particular players. It sounds like they're members of her extended family.

A few seasons back, Alice and my younger son Isaac decided that she would teach him to knit while they watched the World Series together. I'm not sure how this came about. Perhaps Isaac set the goal to knit a hat for me at this particular juncture because a few weeks earlier I had mentioned how Japanese samurai once knit and sold split-toed socks.

I can't say which teams were playing, or how many games and days Alice and Isaac spent knitting and watching the

Series, but at the end of it all, Isaac had half-knit a rather knotty hat. Though he is a skilled carpenter and adept with his hands, the end of the Series marked the end of his knitting career. He told me he couldn't believe how difficult and tedious knitting is.

"It's not for everybody," I told him.

I met a woman named Heather who said it's worth it to teach anybody to knit, even if they give up because it's too hard. "They learn how much effort goes into making even the simplest item, and that makes them truly appreciate the knitted presents you give them."

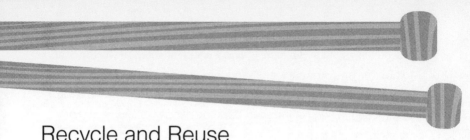

Recycle and Reuse

Last year I collected used sweaters, unraveled them, washed the yarn, and rolled balls for new treasures. When I tired of that, I culled from Goodwill men's silk ties in racy colors. I ignored the tags and washed all the ties in the machine, unseamed them, ironed them, and cut them into raw-edged strips of somewhat similar widths. At a dollar a pop, the ties were turning into expensive "yarn." What middle-aged man doesn't have never-worn ties hiding in his closet? My husband belongs to a men's group that generously donated to my cause.

I kept different colored strips separated in Ziploc bags and stapled them together to keep the color sequence consistent. I cast twelve stitches onto size 9 needles and knotted the strips together as I knit. The raw edges and knots gave my "decorative scarf" great texture, and the varied colors created my personal version of Ikat knitting. Friends and onlookers loved the look and feel of this project, but would anyone really wear it? I realized I wouldn't. My aim was to knit the scarf to six feet, quit, and find its rightful owner. I was two-thirds toward this goal as I sat knitting and waiting for Totsy, my hairdresser, to give me my usual hack-it-off-and-trim-around-the-ears haircut. Totsy is a quiet woman in her forties with bright red hair and a broad smile. She rubbed the end of the scarf between her palms and said, "My daughter would love this!" Totsy's eighteen-year-old had just returned from an extended trip to Ireland where she had learned to knit. Now she was knitting regularly and looking for unique knitted items. "Maria, you could sell these things," Totsy said. "In fact, I want to buy one for my daughter." I realized I couldn't price all the hours I'd spent on this experiment. I said I would think about it. By my next haircut, I had finished the scarf and come up with a solution. I gave Totsy the scarf for her daughter's Christmas present, and in return, my next six haircuts would be tip-free.

Increased appetite:
Golden strands with sunset hues
Lush cascading silks

Always New Territory

Through most of my knitting life I was determined to tackle complex projects, thrilled by all challenging stitches and shapes. I was a traditionalist, wanting to produce beautiful yet absolutely practical clothing. Lately, I've found myself more in sync with many young knitters I meet. I'm looking for adventure. I want to knit in wild colors with unusual textures. I love reading patterns for ideas, but I'm less interested in following them. I start with a general concept that unfolds into something unexpected, perhaps even sculptural. On one friend's desk is a bird's nest she knit. In it she tucks small pieces of paper on which she has written current notes and prayers. In this way she honors her inside spirit with personal messages she hides in her knitted nest. No one else sees them. And as her life cycles, she strips out the old prayers and relines her sturdy nest with new ones.

Fiber asks for form
The mind seeks its harmony
Nuzzles in a shape

Playtime

In his poem "Berryman," W. S. Merwin asks his mentor if he can count on anything he writes being good. "If you have to be sure don't write," answers the poet. Similarly, poet Lucille Clifton says, "Poems come out of wonder, not out of knowing." The same is true in knitting. If I must know in advance that I will succeed in a certain way, then I doom myself to hours of tortured anxiety instead of wondrous free play.

Just botched my sweater
     Is there nothing to behold?
All is sacrament

To Celebrate the Self

William Stafford, one of my top ten favorite poets, is reported to have written at least one poem every day of his adult life. Some years ago, interviewer Bill Moyers asked if that rumor was true, and if so, how was Stafford able to do it. Stafford said he did indeed write a poem a day. It was easy. He just lowered his standards. From what I read, Stafford was a modest and ethical man, like my grandfather Sugar. And along with Sug, he holds a place in my pantheon of the "Good Fathers." Though I don't write or knit every day, I have learned to honor my own wild style of disciplined determination. Day by day, I hold to my thread and shape it as well as I can.

The Way It Is

"There's a thread you follow. It goes among

things that change. But it doesn't change.

People wonder about what you are pursuing.

You have to explain about the thread.

But it is hard for others to see.

While you hold it you can't get lost.

Tragedies happen; people get hurt

or die; and you suffer and get old.

Nothing you do can stop time's unfolding.

You don't ever let go of the thread."

—William Stafford

Goodnight Moon

Sometimes I imagine myself back twenty-some years ago with my sons, three and five years old. It is bedtime. We are reading our favorite book, the Margaret Wise Brown 1947 classic, *Goodnight Moon*. We read it every night. And after my boys are tucked and settled, I carry the book with me to my reading chair in the living room. I study Clement Hurd's illustration of the "quiet old lady who was whispering hush." She is a rabbit in a blue dress rocking in soft light, knitting and keeping watch. Two cats spar with the yarn on the floor, the moon shines outside, the fire burns down, and the baby rabbit goes to sleep.

I feel the deep truth of this image more than I can speak or write about it. As I travel through time, over and over again the act of knitting creates nurturing space around, about, inside, and through me. Though the original miracle of my life was knit together in my mother's womb, the ongoing responsibility to care for myself remains in my own hands. And I am grateful that when I needed it most, knitting mothered me.

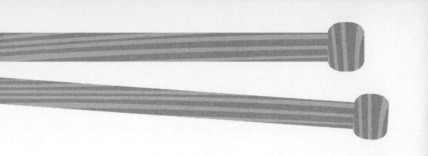

Deep peace of the moon
Deep peace of the quiet knit
Deep peace in softness

Recommended Reading

Knitting into the Mystery: A Guide to the Shawl-Knitting Ministry, Susan
S. Jorgensen and Susan S. Izard. New York: Morehouse Publish-
ing, 2003.

The Knitting Sutra: Craft as Spiritual Practice, Susan Gordan Lydon.
HaperSanFranscico, 1997.

"Yarn" by Kyoko Mori in *The Best American Essays 2004*, Louis
Menand and Robert Atwan. Boston: Houghton Mifflin, 2004.

*Zen & the Art of Knitting: Exploring the Links between Knitting,
Spitituality, and Creativity*, Bernadette Murphy. Avon: Adams
Media, 2002.

Acknowledgments

The writing of this book came to me like a surprise pregnancy. Bryan Robinson, author of more than twenty-five books on human emotions and behavior, suggested we birth a book together. His agent, Sally McMillan, showed our work to editor Kate Epstein. Kate envisioned a book about knitting that would weave prose with haiku. She asked that I try to write it, and Sally deftly negotiated the specifics. Following my surgery, when I doubted I could write this book, beloved Joan Drury gave me two free weeks at Norcroft, the women's writing retreat she created on Lake Superior in Lutsen, Minnesota. The book blossomed there. When I returned home, Kate Epstein decided to leave editing and become an agent. After that, Kirsten Amann worked with me to block my book into what I hope is an inviting shape. These folks deserve extra heartfelt thanks for helping me knit this all together!